D1417434

Today's Superst★rs

Entertainment

Jack Black

By Susan K. Mitchell

Gareth Stevens
Publishing

Please visit our web site at www.garethstevens.com.
For a free color catalog describing our list of high-quality books,
call 1-800-542-2595 (USA) or 1-800-387-3178 (Canada). Our fax: 1-877-542-2596

Library of Congress Cataloging-in-Publication Data
Mitchell, Susan K.
  Jack Black / by Susan K. Mitchell.
      p. cm. — (Today's superstars. Entertainment)
   Includes bibliographical references and index.
   ISBN-13: 978-0-8368-9237-6 (lib. bdg.)
   ISBN-10: 0-8368-9237-2 (lib. bdg.)
      1. Black, Jack, 1969- 2. Actors—United States—Biography. I. Title.
PN2287.B4548M58   2008
792.02'8092—dc22 [B]   2008020736

This edition first published in 2009 by
Gareth Stevens Publishing
A Weekly Reader® Company
1 Reader's Digest Road
Pleasantville, NY 10570-7000 USA

Copyright © 2009 by Gareth Stevens, Inc.
Senior Managing Editor: Lisa M. Herrington
Senior Editor: Brian Fitzgerald
Creative Director: Lisa Donovan
Senior Designer: Keith Plechaty
Production Designer: Cynthia Malaran
Photo Researcher: Kim Babbitt

Photo credits: cover Adolfo Franco/Contour by Getty Images; title page, p. 5
Jesse Grant/Wire Image/Getty Images; p. 6 Frank Micelotta/Getty Images; p. 7
Scott Gries/Getty Images; p. 9 AFP/Getty Images; p. 11 Seth Poppel/Yearbook
Library; p. 13 Nick Ut/AP Images; p. 14 Handout/Getty Images; p. 15 Everett
Collection; p. 16 20th Century Fox Film Corp./courtesy Everett Collection;
p. 18 Paramount/courtesy Everett Collection; p. 20 Dreamworks/courtesy
Everett Collection; p. 22 Universal/courtesy Everett Collection; p. 23 Everett
Collection; p. 24 Paramount/courtesy Everett Collection; p. 25 Tim Mosenfelder/
Getty Images; p. 26 Donato Sardella/Getty Images; p. 27 New Line Cinema/
courtesy Everett Collection; p. 28 Frazer Harrison/AMA/Getty Images.

Printed in the United States

1 2 3 4 5 6 7 8 9 10 09 08

Contents

Words in the glossary appear in **bold** type the first time they are used in the text.

Chapter 1 King of the World

In November 2006, a crowd gathered outside Grauman's Chinese Theatre in Hollywood, California. All eyes were on two men strutting down the red carpet. They wore huge gold crowns on their heads. They wore royal robes and carried scepters in their hands. The men were not kings, however. They were Jack Black and Kyle Gass, otherwise known as the rock band Tenacious D. The two were at the **premiere** of their movie *Tenacious D in The Pick of Destiny.*

Dressing up like a king is just the kind of outrageous behavior that fans have come to expect from Jack Black. People see him as self-confident — and a little bit of an oddball. His film characters usually have some of that same personality.

Jack has played a slacker substitute teacher with dreams of being a rock star. He has also starred as an out-of-shape monk who is convinced he can be a wrestler. And Tenacious D's bizarre, hilarious songs could only come from a twisted mind like Jack's.

A Legend in His Own Mind

Jack loves to pretend to be a **cocky**, self-centered guy. He often tells reporters how awesome he is. He calls Tenacious D "the greatest band on Earth." Of course, it's all a big joke. Jack never takes himself too seriously. That's what fans love about him.

Jack dressed as a king for the premiere of the Tenacious D movie. Kyle Gass said Jack was the "king of rock" and he was "the king of roll."

In 2008, Jack (left) and Orlando Bloom (right) got the longest sliming in Kids' Choice Awards' history.

Slime Time Favorite

Jack's roles in movies such as *Shark Tale*, *School of Rock*, and *Nacho Libre* have made him a favorite with younger fans. Those films—plus his zany personality—also made him a natural choice to host the Nickelodeon Kids' Choice Awards.

Jack first hosted the show in 2006. He jokingly called it "the greatest performance in the history of television." Jack was back in 2008 and promised to be even better. He joked that he spent an entire year training for the show! Whatever he did must have worked. More viewers tuned in to the show than any other in Kids' Choice Awards' history.

Basic Black

Jack does not see himself as *just* an actor or *just* a musician. "I'm an entertainer," he told *Entertainment Weekly.* "You don't know what I'm gonna do [next]." Jack's success in both fields is connected. The popularity of Tenacious D helped him get better acting roles. Later, his acting success attracted more fans to his band.

Still, his success has been a long time in the making. At first, Jack took any small role he could get. Now he gets paid millions to star in a movie. His band now performs for thousands of fans instead of hundreds. It is exactly the kind of attention Jack always dreamed of as a kid.

Kyle and Jack performed at the 2001 MTV Video Music Awards.

Chapter 2

Center of Attention

Thomas Jack Black Jr. was born on August 28, 1969. Until he was 10 years old, Jack lived in Hermosa Beach, California. Both of his parents, Jack Sr. and Judith, were rocket scientists. They worked with space satellites. Jack's mother even worked on the Hubble Space Telescope. "I didn't inherit any of their brainpower," Jack told *Newsweek*. "But I have the power to rock. They're rocket scientists. I'm a *rock* scientist."

Fact File

As a kid, Jack sometimes kept wires hidden in his sleeves. He would let the wires fall out as he walked around so that people might think he was a robot!

Acting Out Early

Jack grew up in a big family. He had four older stepsiblings. He was always competing for attention at home. At school, Jack was considered the class clown. He would do just about anything to get noticed.

Big Changes

Life took a huge turn for Jack when he was 10. His parents went through a bad divorce. Their breakup was very upsetting for Jack. After the divorce, he moved with his mother to Culver City, California.

Jack's need for attention led him to acting. At age 13, he got his first job. It was a commercial for the video game *Pitfall*. "I knew that if my friends saw me on TV, it would be the answer to all my prayers. Because then ... everyone would know I was awesome," Jack told *Newsweek*. "And I *was* awesome—for three days."

Jack still loves being in the spotlight. In 2004, he posed for photographers at a film festival in France.

Trouble on the Rise

A few days of fame weren't enough to satisfy Jack. His need for attention took a downward turn. By the eighth grade, he was hanging out with a bad crowd. He started skipping school and getting into trouble. Jack's bad behavior continued in high school. The last straw came when he stole money from his mother's purse. When Jack was 15, his mother sent him to a school for troubled teens.

Helping Hands

Jack's new school was called Poseidon School. The counselors there got him the help he needed. They encouraged him to talk about his problems. Acting became a bigger part of Jack's life. It helped him focus his energy in a positive way.

Jack and the Box

Jack's love of video games didn't end after childhood. He still spends hours playing video games on his Xbox. Kyle Gass told *People* magazine, "He loves video games so much that when he's playing, I say he's *working*."

Jack has even been *in* video games. In 2008, he voiced the main character of the video game *Brutal Legend*. "The Metal," by Tenacious D, is one of the songs in the top-selling game *Guitar Hero III: Legends of Rock*.

At Crossroads School, Jack starred in a production of the play *Pippin*.

At Crossroads

Soon, Jack switched to a performing arts high school called Crossroads. There, he continued to study acting. Jack graduated in 1987 and enrolled at the University of California, Los Angeles (UCLA). While in college, he joined a theater group called the Actors' Gang. Being a part of the group helped Jack sharpen his acting skills. He also made connections there that would jump-start his career.

Fact File

Jack met Tanya Haden when they were students at Crossroads. They met again as adults and were married in 2006.

Chapter 3 Succeeding as a Loser

Jack dropped out of college after less than two years. He wanted to pursue acting full-time. Jack stayed involved with the Actors' Gang. There he met Kyle Gass. At first, the two struggling actors hated each other. "We were archenemies," Jack told *People* magazine. "We both wanted to be the musician of the [acting] group." A shared love of comedy and music, however, soon changed the "enemies" into best friends.

Being a part of the Actors' Gang also helped Jack get his first big break. In 1992, he landed a small role in the movie comedy *Bob Roberts*. The movie was directed by and starred Tim Robbins, the founder of the Actors' Gang.

Busy Black

For the next few years, Jack took any role he could get. He landed small parts on TV shows, such as *Life Goes On* and *The X Files*. Jack also took minor roles in *Enemy of the State, Waterworld,* and other films.

Breaking Out the Rock

While Jack kept busy acting, he started a side project with Kyle Gass. In 1994, the duo formed the comedy rock band Tenacious D. They started performing at local comedy clubs. Their act **spoofed** the heavy metal bands of the 1970s and 1980s. The crowds loved them!

Before long, the band caught the attention of Hollywood **producers**. In 1997, Tenacious D landed its own show on HBO. Three years later, the duo signed a recording contract with Epic Records.

Kyle and Jack love to joke around, but they are serious about their music.

Jack got a chance to show his singing talent in *High Fidelity*.

Perfecting Imperfection

Jack's crazed energy on his HBO show caught the eye of **director** Stephen Frears and actor John Cusack. Frears cast Jack in his first major movie role in *High Fidelity*. Jack got the part without an **audition**. Until then, all his film roles had been minor. He was not sure he could succeed in a major role. Jack almost turned down the offer.

Luckily, that brief lack of confidence didn't keep Jack from taking the part. Cusack was the star of the film. But Jack stole the show as Barry, a slacker record-store employee.

Original Rock Mockery

Jack and Kyle Gass were not the first actors to form a comedy rock band. In the late 1970s, actors Michael McKean, Harry Shearer, and Christopher Guest formed Spinal Tap. In 1984, the trio released a movie about the fake rock band called *This Is Spinal Tap*. Today the film is hailed as a comedy classic. One famous line from the movie sums up what it's like to be a comedy rock band: "It's such a fine line between stupid and clever."

Spinal Tap was a big influence on Jack. "The movie *Spinal Tap* rocked my world," he said in an interview. "They really nailed how dumb rock can be."

The members of Spinal Tap (from left): Harry Shearer, Christopher Guest (sitting), and Michael McKean.

Gwyneth Paltrow
and Jack starred
as unlikely lovers
in *Shallow Hal*.

Ready for Takeoff

Jack's career started to take off. After *High Fidelity*, he got offers for bigger roles with bigger paychecks. Jack got his first part as a leading man in *Shallow Hal*. He starred opposite Gwyneth Paltrow in his first romantic film. *Shallow Hal* was not a hit with **critics**, but it made more than $70 million.

Jack's musical career was also soaring. His band released its first album, titled *Tenacious D*, in 2001. The album went on to sell more than 1 million copies.

Fact File

In 1999, Jack starred in a TV show called *Heat Vision and Jack*. He played an ex-astronaut who had superpowers. Owen Wilson played his sidekick, a talking motorcycle! The show never aired.

Chapter 4   Rocking to the Top

In 2003, Jack's acting career reached an all-time high. That year, he starred as Dewey Finn in *School of Rock*. The character is a frustrated rocker who gets kicked out of his band. Desperate for money, Dewey lies his way into a substitute-teaching job. At the school, he transforms a group of 10-year-old students into a rock band.

Mike White wrote the script for *School of Rock*. He is Jack's good friend and former neighbor. White created the part of Dewey with Jack in mind. "I was born to play this part," Jack told *Newsweek*. "Everything about it lines up perfectly with my strengths."

Fact File

The kids in Jack's band in *School of Rock* were actual musicians. None of them had any acting experience.

A Star on the Rise

Audiences loved *School of Rock*. The film was number one at the box office during its first week. It went on to make more than $130 million worldwide. At the time, *School of Rock* was Jack's most successful movie. The film was also a hit with critics. Jack was nominated for a Golden Globe award for his role.

In *School of Rock*, Jack got to combine his love of acting and music.

Shark Success

Jack's good luck continued with his next film. He starred with Will Smith, Robert DeNiro, and Renée Zellweger in the animated hit *Shark Tale*. Jack played Lenny, a great white shark that doesn't eat meat. *Shark Tale* opened at number one at the box office in October 2004.

Same Old Story

All of a sudden, Jack was a **mainstream** movie star. One thing that had not changed, however, was the type of roles he was offered. In script after script, Jack was asked to read the part of the lovable loser. That would soon change.

Pulling His Weight

Jack has always been on the heavy side, and he is comfortable with the way he looks. "I don't get hung up on weight," he says. In public, he often jokes about his size. He's not shy about showing off his belly in his films or at awards shows.

Jack wouldn't change his appearance just to get a part in a movie. "If someone asked me to lose, say, 30 pounds for a film, it would have to be an awfully cool part," he says. "And nothing's coming to mind right now."

Jack says he loves doing voice work for films because he can just roll out of bed and go to work!

Mighty Animated

With his wild eyebrows and facial expressions, Jack has an almost cartoonish quality. It's only natural that he has done voice work for animated movies. Lenny in *Shark Tale* wasn't his first 'toon role. Jack provided the voice of Zeke, a saber-toothed tiger, in the 2002 hit movie *Ice Age*.

"Since I saw *Aladdin*, with Robin Williams [as the genie], I wanted to do a cartoon character," he said. In 2008, Jack played yet another lovable cartoon character. He starred in *Kung Fu Panda* as Po (above), a chubby panda with less-than-superb kung fu skills.

Chapter 5

Kong and Beyond

In 2004, Jack took his first starring role in a dramatic movie. He played the part of movie director Carl Denham in *King Kong*. The film was a remake of the classic film from 1933. In the film, Denham takes his movie cast and crew to the fictional Skull Island. There, they **encounter** the legendary 25-foot-tall gorilla, King Kong. Denham sees a chance for fame and fortune. He captures Kong and takes him back to New York City. The destruction that follows is movie history.

Jack had wanted to work with *King Kong* director Peter Jackson for a long time. Jackson had directed the very successful *Lord of the Rings* films. When the part in *King Kong* came up, Jack jumped at it.

Jackson and Black

Peter Jackson was equally eager to work with Jack. He had wanted to work with Jack since seeing him in *High Fidelity*. "He's a smart and **versatile** actor blessed with an abundance of energy and charm," Jackson told the *Hollywood Reporter*.

The role was very different from anything Jack had ever done. Carl Denham was not only a serious character but also a **villain**. Critics were surprised by how well Jack handled the role. He showed he wasn't just a comedic actor.

Peter Jackson discusses a scene with Jack during the filming of *King Kong*.

In *King Kong*, the giant gorilla battles airplanes from atop the Empire State Building in New York. It is one of the most famous scenes in movie history.

Going Ape

King Kong is the most famous movie monster of all time. The original *King Kong* was a huge hit in 1933. The special effects in the film don't seem very advanced today. At the time, however, audiences had never seen anything like it.

The makers of the original *King Kong* used stop-motion photography. They took a photo of a small model of a gorilla. Then they repositioned the model and took another photo. They had to repeat this process hundreds of times just to get a few seconds of film!

The filming process for the 2005 remake was very different. King Kong was created using computer-generated images (CGI). For scenes with the giant ape, Jack and the rest of the cast acted against a blank screen. The filmmakers added King Kong and most of the scenery later on.

Gorilla-Sized Hit

King Kong was by far the most expensive movie of Jack's career. It cost more than $200 million to make! It also made more money than any of his other movies. *King Kong* has made more than $550 million worldwide. The film was also nominated for four Oscars, the top awards for movies.

Back to Being Jack

Jack's performance in *King Kong* did not put an end to his goofy roles. In 2006, he starred in *Nacho Libre*. He played a half-Latino monk who wrestles in "stretchy pants" to raise money for an orphanage.

Jack called *Nacho Libre* "the most original movie I've been in."

Rocking the House That Jack Built

Later in 2006, Jack and Kyle Gass released the film *Tenacious D in The Pick of Destiny*. They also took their act on the road for their first worldwide tour. In the early days, Tenacious D played in small clubs. The show was just Kyle and Jack playing **acoustic guitars**.

Their new tour was entirely different. The stage was set up to look like Kyle's living room. Later in the show, Kyle and Jack played in front of flames and smoking volcanoes. They were joined by a full rock band. The duo played to packed crowds in huge arenas, such as Madison Square Garden in New York.

Fact File

Jack keeps strange hours. He usually stays up all night watching movies or playing video games. "I sleep from 6 A.M. to 2 in the afternoon," he told *Entertainment Weekly*.

Black Never Fades

Jack wasn't just reaching new heights as a musician. Filmmakers had not forgotten his performance in *King Kong*. He began to get offers for a wide variety of roles. Jack played romantic roles in his next two films. In 2006, he starred with Kate Winslet in *The Holiday*. The following year, he starred with Jennifer Jason Leigh in *Margot at the Wedding*.

Family Man

Romance was blossoming in real life for Jack as well. In March 2006, he married Tanya Haden. The couple's son Samuel was born later that year. In May 2008, Tanya gave birth to their second son. Jack loves being a dad. He says it hasn't changed his choices in movie roles yet. "If I were a tough action dude … I might have to rethink my career," Jack jokes. "But luckily I don't!"

Tanya and Sam joined Jack at a charity event in November 2007. Jack had dyed his hair blond for his role in *Tropic Thunder*.

Staying Busy

Jack was busy at home with his new family. He was also juggling more movie projects than ever before. In 2008, he returned to his comedy roots in three films. In *Be Kind Rewind*, he played a zany guy whose brain is magnetized. His magnetic brain accidentally erases all the videotapes in his friend's video store. Jack's character and his friend remake the movies one by one by themselves.

Jack also starred with Dustin Hoffman and Angelina Jolie in the animated hit *Kung Fu Panda*. His last film of the year was *Tropic Thunder*. He starred with Ben Stiller in the spoof of war movies.

Jack has many friends and fans in the rock world. One of his famous friends is Dave Grohl (right) of Foo Fighters.

Still Rocking

Jack is equally committed to his movie career and his band. Between movies, he works with Kyle Gass on new Tenacious D songs. It's hard to imagine where he finds the energy to be a movie star, a rock star, and a family man. One thing is for sure, though: Jack knows what pushes him to succeed. "A lot of my motivation and what I've accomplished is just out of the fear that I'm going to end up back at my mom's house," he jokes. As long as he keeps acting and rocking, Jack won't have to worry about that!

Time Line

1969 Thomas Jack Black Jr. is born on August 28, 1969, in Santa Monica, California.

1982 Appears in his first commercial, for the Atari video game *Pitfall*.

1992 Appears in his first film, *Bob Roberts*.

1994 Forms the band Tenacious D with Kyle Gass.

2000 Has his breakthrough role as a record-store clerk in *High Fidelity*.

2001 Stars in *Shallow Hal*; Tenacious D releases its first album, titled *Tenacious D*.

2003 Stars as Dewey Finn in *School of Rock*.

2005 Stars as Carl Denham in *King Kong*.

2006 Stars in *Nacho Libre*, *Tenacious D in The Pick of Destiny*, and *The Holiday*; marries Tanya Haden in March; son Samuel is born in June; launches a world tour with Tenacious D.

2008 Stars in *Be Kind Rewind*, *Kung Fu Panda*, and *Tropic Thunder*.

# Glossary

acoustic guitars — guitars that are not plugged in to amplifiers

audition — a tryout for a role in a movie, play, or TV show

cocky — overly self-confident

critics — in entertainment, people whose job is to give their opinions about movies, TV shows, or music

director — a person who is in charge during the filming of a movie or TV show

encounter — to come face-to-face with an enemy

mainstream — popularly accepted by many people

premiere — the first public showing of a movie

producers — people who get the money and organize the people to make a movie or TV show

spoofed — made fun of or imitated in a humorous way

versatile — talented in many ways

villain — an evil character in a movie, play, TV show, or video game

To Find Out More

Books

Kung Fu Panda: The Junior Novel. Susan Korman
(HarperEntertainment, 2008)

Movie Acting. Making Movies (series). Geoffrey M. Horn
(Gareth Stevens, 2007)

DVDs

King Kong (Universal, 2006)*

Nacho Libre (Paramount, 2006)

School of Rock (Paramount, 2004)*

Shark Tale (Dreamworks Animation, 2005)

Rated PG-13

Web Sites

www.kungfupanda.com
Play games, get downloads, and meet the martial arts
masters of *Kung Fu Panda.*

www.schoolofrockmovie.com
The official *School of Rock* web site has interviews with the
cast, clips of songs from the film, and games to test your
knowledge of rock.

Index

About the Author

Susan K. Mitchell has always loved books, movies, and music. She is the author of more than 15 nonfiction chapter books for young readers. Susan has also written several children's picture books. She lives near Houston, Texas, with her husband, two daughters, a dog, and two cats. She dedicates this book to Emily and Rachel—who ROCK!